Original title:
Netted Jots Among the Dragon Mull

Author: Swan Charm

ISBN HARDBACK: 978-1-80562-658-9
ISBN PAPERBACK: 978-1-80564-179-7

Embers of Memory in the Forest's Heart

In twilight's hush, where shadows creep,
The whispers of the past do seep.
Through tangled roots and ancient trees,
The forest breathes, a tale of ease.

Where laughter danced in sunlit beams,
And shared the warmth of secret dreams,
Each leaf a note, each branch a song,
In memories, we all belong.

The ferns unfold like gentle sighs,
As time unveils its soft goodbyes.
Beneath the arch of emerald skies,
The heart of stillness never lies.

Yet embers glow in softest night,
A spark of joy, a trace of light.
With every step, we find a clue,
In shadows deep, the past rings true.

So heed the tales the forest weaves,
In every rustle, every breeze.
For in its heart, we come to see,
The ties that bind you back to me.

Whimsy in an Elven Glade

In the glade where shadows dance,
Whispers float on breezes bright.
Elves laugh soft, in silver light,
Their laughter weaves a spell of chance.

Beneath the boughs, a secret brook,
Sings of tales both old and new.
With every glance, a spark of dew,
Each hidden glance, a knowing look.

The ferns nod gently in the breeze,
As petals swirl in joyful flight.
Dancing stars adorn the night,
While crickets play with perfect ease.

Old oaks stand with watchful grace,
Guardians of the glade's delight.
In their arms, dreams take flight,
A tapestry of time and space.

Notes from the Dreamweaver's Book

In a tome where wishes dwell,
Each page glimmers with desire.
Thoughts take flight, like sparks of fire,
In dreams that weave a magic spell.

With ink of starlight, stories flow,
Of realms where shadows softly play.
Each line a bridge, a whispered say,
Of hopes that dance with joy and glow.

The Dreamweaver's quill moves swift,
Bringing forth what hearts conceal.
Through every line, you dare to feel,
A treasure trove, a priceless gift.

In twilight's hush, the whispers rise,
Shimmering tales of love and loss.
To journey forth, no matter cost,
A world where every dream belies.

The Enchanted Path of Secrets

Winding through the ancient trees,
The path of secrets softly calls.
With echoes of the past it sprawls,
As winds carry unspoken pleas.

Moonlight glints on stones so old,
Each step a tale, a life untold.
With every turn, the air grows bold,
A promise wrapped in shimmered gold.

Beneath the canopy so wide,
The whispers of the forest sigh.
In shadows where the phantoms lie,
Each secret watched from deep inside.

Follow where the fireflies gleam,
Their glow a map, a guiding light.
Through dusk and dawn, from day to night,
The enchanted path reveals a dream.

Murmurs between the Twisted Roots

Among the roots where secrets dwell,
Murmurs echo through the earth.
In whispered tones, they share their worth,
Of ages past, of time's great swell.

The tangled limbs, a story spun,
Of laughter, sorrow, life and strife.
Each winding twist, a breath of life,
Beneath the cover of the sun.

In the twilight, shadows creep,
Stirring tales of ancient lore.
An unseen world begins to soar,
As night descends and dreams take leap.

From hollow trunks, old voices rise,
With wisdom held in nature's clasp.
In roots entwined, their truths are rasped,
A melody beneath the skies.

Whispers from the Cresting Shadows

In the woods where silence lies,
Softly breathe the ancient sighs.
Echoes of the night unfold,
Secrets in the dark, untold.

Beneath the branches, shadows creep,
Guarding dreams that dare to leap.
Misty veils and moonlit trails,
Stories woven in the gales.

Gentle whispers kiss the trees,
Carrying the past like leaves.
With every rustle, tales rewind,
In the twilight, magic's kind.

A figure dances, cloaked in night,
Casting spells in dimmest light.
The heart of mystery beats near,
In shadows' dance, all is clear.

So listen close, the world will speak,
In every hush, the brave will seek.
From the cresting shadows' lore,
Carry forth the dreams we soar.

Legends in the Cinders' Glow

Fires crackle, embers spark,
Whispers woven in the dark.
In the glow, where tales ignite,
Legends live in dead of night.

Cinders cradle dreams of old,
With every flicker, stories told.
Bravery wrapped in smoke and flame,
Heroes rise, though none the same.

Glow of wisdom in the ash,
Fables born with every flash.
From the warmth, heartbeats align,
In the firelight, fates entwine.

Ashes speak of battles fought,
In their depths, the lessons sought.
Threads of time in shadows blend,
From cinders' glow, our journeys mend.

Lift your voice, and join the throng,
Sing with me this ancient song.
Legends flicker, spirits flow,
In our hearts, the cinders glow.

Murmurs of Fables Found in the Wilds

In wilds where the whispers roam,
Lies a story, far from home.
Each rustle feeds the vibrant lore,
Nature's heartbeat, evermore.

From the brook to the soaring tree,
Fables dwell in harmony.
Footfalls echo on the ground,
In the shadows, magic's found.

Hushed voices ride the gentle breeze,
Carrying lore across the leaves.
Every creature knows the song,
In the wilds, where we belong.

Murmurs travel far and wide,
Secrets cloaked in nature's tide.
In the twilight, creatures weave,
The fables that we dare believe.

So journey forth, let spirits guide,
In whispered tales, we'll confide.
The wilds are rich with stories spun,
In every heart, a world begun.

The Glimpse of the Celestial Thread

When stars align in velvet night,
A tapestry of pure delight.
In the silence, wishes twine,
Threads of fate, so fine, divine.

Celestial bodies dance above,
Guiding dreams, wrapped in love.
Every shimmer, a path unfolds,
In the cosmos, truth beholds.

Woven in the starlit gleam,
Is the heartbeat of a dream.
Glimpses passed through time and space,
Reveal our souls' eternal grace.

Each twinkling light a story cast,
Drawn from future, present, past.
Follow where the stardust leads,
In these threads, our spirit feeds.

So gaze upon the heavens high,
Let your spirit learn to fly.
In the vastness, wisdom thread,
Find yourself where dreams are spread.

Beneath the Canopy of Fire

Beneath the canopy of fire,
Where whispers dance on winds of fate,
The embers glow with fierce desire,
In twilight's grasp, we contemplate.

The branches sway, a gentle sigh,
As starlit dreams begin to weave,
The secrets held where shadows lie,
In hearts that long to dare and believe.

A flicker here, a shimmer bright,
The night unfolds its softest threads,
As visions spark in fleeting light,
And hopes ignite where courage treads.

With every crackle, every flame,
The forest hums a timeless tune,
In unity, we share the name,
Of passion born beneath the moon.

Oh, listen close, the spirits call,
In every rustle, every breath,
A harmony that binds us all,
As fire dances, defying death.

Songs of the Emberbound Grove

In emberbound grove where shadows sway,
A song of old begins to rise,
With notes that chase the night away,
And paint the dark with starlit skies.

The branches hum, a melody,
Each leaf aflame with secret tales,
Of dreams that spark eternally,
In whispers soft as midnight gales.

Each tiny flame, a beacon bright,
Their dances weave through twilight's seam,
And guide the lost with tender light,
To find their path, to chase a dream.

The echoes of forgotten lore,
In every creak and crack of wood,
Invite us to explore once more,
The magic where we once then stood.

So linger here, 'neath ancient trees,
Let every breath a new tune bring,
For in this grove, the heart finds ease,
And in our souls, the fire sings.

Secrets in the Shaded Hollow

In shaded hollow, secrets lie,
Where sunlight fades and shadows grow,
A world away from busy sighs,
In whispers soft, the breezes flow.

The ancient stones, they seem to speak,
Of journeys taken, paths divine,
With every crack, a tale unique,
In silent echoes, history entwines.

Among the ferns and moss so green,
The magic waits, both bold and shy,
In hidden glades where few have been,
A refuge for the wandering eye.

Here wildflowers bloom, then fade,
With colors bright, yet fleeting grace,
Each bloom a promise, softly laid,
In nature's warm and sweet embrace.

So raise your heart and listen close,
To murmurs lost in twilight's sweep,
For in this place, where time can doze,
The secrets told are yours to keep.

Shadows of the Wyrm's Lair

In shadows deep, the wyrm does dwell,
A legend forged in fire and fear,
With scales of night and breath of hell,
The whispers speak of destiny near.

The lair echoes with tales of old,
Of brave souls who dared to stand tall,
With hearts aflame, their spirits bold,
In darkness bright, they answered the call.

The flicker of tales, a guiding light,
To shine through fears, to pierce the gloom,
For those who seek, both day and night,
Will find their strength amidst the doom.

With every thrum of beating wings,
The air is thick with dreams and dread,
A battle fought, a melody sings,
Of courage found where angels tread.

So venture forth, if you are brave,
To face the wyrm and claim your fate,
For in this lair, the light will wave,
And legends live, forever great.

Floating Thoughts Beneath the Arching Boughs

Beneath the branches, whispers sigh,
As gentle breezes softly fly.
Dreams flutter like a feathered wisp,
In nature's cradle, tranquil grip.

A tapestry of green unfolds,
With stories waiting to be told.
Each shadow dances, light entwines,
In this sanctuary, peace aligns.

Thoughts drift like clouds, free and vast,
Moments linger, no need for haste.
The heart beats with the rhythm slow,
In this haven where wildflowers grow.

Echoes of laughter in the air,
Brought forth by those who wander there.
Nature cradles them with her song,
In the stillness, they all belong.

So let your spirit wander free,
Under arching boughs, you'll see.
A world alive with magic's glow,
In this realm where thoughts may flow.

Stitches of Serenity in a Dreamweaver's Field

In the dreamweaver's field, time slows,
Where the gentle river flows.
Brilliant colors dance in light,
Whispers of calm in the night.

Each petal stitched with care and grace,
A tapestry in nature's embrace.
Here, dreams are woven, hearts align,
In fields of peace, all will be fine.

The hush of twilight, soft and deep,
Calls to the weary, beckons sleep.
With every sigh, a blessing finds,
In starlit whispers, ease unwinds.

Here pause and ponder, breathe it in,
The stillness wraps like a soft spin.
In each heartbeat, serenity's thread,
Awakens colors long since fled.

So drift through these fields, loose and free,
In harmony, let your spirit be.
Stitch by stitch, in twilight's glow,
Find the peace that you long to know.

The Heartbeat of Nature's Chorus

In the woods where silence thrives,
Nature's heartbeat comes alive.
The rustle of leaves, a sacred hymn,
Each pulse, a promise, soft and dim.

Sunlight filters through the trees,
Whispers carried on the breeze.
Every creature sings a note,
In unity, a healing throat.

The brook babbles secrets old,
Of adventures untold, bold.
In this grand symphony, find your place,
Feel the rhythm, nature's grace.

With every roar and every sigh,
The heartbeat echoes, never shy.
In moments still, be aware,
Life's magic lingers everywhere.

So stand beneath the endless sky,
And let your spirit learn to fly.
Join the chorus, wild and free,
In the heartbeat of all you see.

Glimpses into the Mystic Veil

In twilight's glow, a veil appears,
Glimmers of magic, ancient years.
Softly calling, whispers low,
Into the realm where dreamers go.

Shadows play in the moonlight's grace,
Each flicker hints of a hidden place.
The world beneath the stars so bright,
Offers secrets wrapped in night.

From the depths of silence, visions rise,
With every breath, the soul complies.
In mystic moments, hearts will stir,
Finding truths in the gentle blur.

The veil, it beckons, tender call,
Whispers of wonder, inviting all.
In the dance of dreams, be unconfined,
Discover the treasures that intertwine.

So take a step beyond the veil,
Where every heartbeat tells a tale.
In the mystery, let your spirit sail,
With glimpses of magic in the trail.

Silhouettes of the Subtle Wind

In whispers soft, the shadows weave,
The gentle touch of evening's grieve.
A rustling sigh, a fleeting glance,
Beneath the stars, the dreamers dance.

A wisp of fog, a flickering light,
Guides hidden paths through the twilight.
In every breeze, a story spun,
Of secret realms where time is none.

Faint echoes call from far away,
A soft retreat, as night holds sway.
Each phantom shape begins to blend,
With all the dreams that night can send.

Through quiet nights, the spirits play,
In the cool embrace where shadows stay.
The subtle wind, a bard so fine,
Whispers truths on fragile line.

And as the dawn begins to rise,
The silhouettes greet morning skies.
With every gust, a promise made,
That life and dreams shall not soon fade.

The Cauldron of Echoing Tales

Deep in the woods, where magic brews,
A cauldron stirs with ancient views.
The tales it tells, both grim and bright,
Woven in strands of dark and light.

Each bubbling drop a whisper shared,
Stories of mortals who once dared.
The flickering flame, a guiding hand,
Through murky depths of time's demand.

With herbs of fate and roots of dreams,
It steeps the hopes of silent screams.
A potion brewed in night's embrace,
Reflects the truth of every face.

Through swirling mists, the visions dance,
A fleeting glimpse of fate's strange chance.
In every sip, a life unfolds,
In echoes deep, the saga holds.

As shadows wane and light draws near,
The cauldron's song is all we hear.
In each tale spun, in every breath,
Lies the power of life and death.

Fragments of an Otherworldly Tapestry

Threads of silver, woven tight,
In realms beyond our sight.
A tapestry of stars and dreams,
Where nothing's quite as it seems.

Colors blend in cosmic dance,
Inviting all to take a chance.
Each fragment holds a tale unique,
In silence loud, the starlit speak.

Soar through galaxies, unfurl,
Unlock the mysteries they twirl.
In every stitch, a whispered cheer,
For distant worlds we long to near.

Time and space twist like a song,
In harmony, where we belong.
With every thread, the past unveiled,
A thousand stories intertwined, detailed.

In this grand loom of fate's design,
Each heart a thread, each soul a sign.
As daylight fades to twilight's glow,
The tapestry whispers what we know.

Vignettes from the Celestials' Hideaway

In a glade where starlights play,
The celestials weave night from day.
With laughter bright, they build their homes,
Among the stars where starlight roams.

Every whisper, a silver ray,
Guides the lost upon their way.
A sanctuary of dreams untold,
Wrapped in the stories of the bold.

Beneath the moon's tender gaze,
They dance in light's enchanting haze.
With every twirl, they cast their fate,
In worlds where love and hope await.

The breezes carry their sweet refrain,
Through spaces vast where they remain.
In secret corners, magic thrives,
As every heart in rhythm strives.

So listen close, for they invite,
Your dreams to wander through the night.
In the hideaway, all hearts reveal,
The whispers of the night, so real.

Reflections in the Enchanted Stream

In glimmers bright, the water flows,
Whispers of time, where magic grows.
Frogs croak soft, beneath the trees,
Secrets danced on gentle breeze.

Rippling echoes of laughter past,
Captured smiles that forever last.
Waves of wonder, stories unfold,
In the stream, hearts brave and bold.

Moonlight weaves through willow's grace,
A haunting tune, a fleeting trace.
With every splash, a wish taken,
Fragile dreams, but never shaken.

In twilight's cloak, the shadows play,
Hope and fear in soft array.
Magic stirs a tender song,
In the stream, where souls belong.

Reflection glows in pearly light,
Illumining the depths of night.
A charm concealed in liquid hue,
Awaits the heart that dares pursue.

Shadows of the Mystic Expanse

Veils of night stretch far and wide,
In dreams that ebb like ocean tide.
Stars blink softly, whispers sent,
Across the dark, where hopes are bent.

Winds carry tales of past and far,
Beneath the gaze of the guiding star.
Echoes call with voices clear,
In the shadows, cast by fear.

Misty paths weave through the night,
Drawing seekers towards the light.
Each step taken, magic swirls,
Unraveled fates, where mystery unfurls.

In twilight's breath, history sighs,
Lost adventures beneath the skies.
From darkness blooms the whispered truth,
In shadows played, dreams find their youth.

Stars will guide, and shadows weave,
Threads of fate that we conceive.
In the mystic expanse of time,
Hearts will echo, tendrils rhyme.

Dreams Entangled in Verdant Hues

In the heart of emerald glens,
Where sunlight skips, and magic bends.
Dreams lie nestled in the leaves,
Whispers soft, in twilight eaves.

Mossy paths and flowers bright,
Guide the wanderers in delight.
Butterflies dance with laughter pure,
In nature's charm, they find their cure.

With every breeze, a tale is spun,
Underneath the golden sun.
Woven threads of light and shade,
In verdant hues, memories fade.

Branches sway, a lullaby sings,
Of forgotten hopes and fleeting things.
In the glade, dreams intertwine,
In whispers cool, they gently shine.

Here, where shadows kiss the ground,
Magic breathes without a sound.
Nature cradles every prayer,
In verdant hues, dreams dance in air.

Fantasies Caught in Celestial Traps

Beneath the dome where stars align,
Fantasies flicker, bright and fine.
Caught in webs of shimmering night,
Dreams entwined in celestial light.

Comets trace their ancient paths,
Whispers soft of fate and maths.
In the dance of the cosmic show,
Wishes soar where few would go.

Galaxies spin, their secrets kept,
In the silence, hope is swept.
Infinity holds its breath in grace,
While dreams explore the vastness of space.

Constellations beckon, winds of time,
Each star a tale, sublime and prime.
In orbits locked, the heart does yearn,
For the fantasies, destined to return.

Caught in traps of twilight's gaze,
Fleeting moments, a dreamy haze.
The universe whispers, soft and clear,
In celestial realms, dreams persevere.

Lullabies of the Wandering Spirits

In the night, whispers roam free,
Lost souls hum their ancient decree.
Crickets play a soft serenade,
Echoing where the moonlight swayed.

Stars twinkle like distant dreams,
Bathed in the glow of silvery beams.
Wandering spirits find their grace,
In the universal, boundless space.

Through the trees, a gentle sigh,
Breezes carry the sweet goodbye.
Feathers fall, like memories dear,
Each echoing softly, crystal clear.

A lullaby for every heart,
Guided by the night's quiet art.
With every note, a story unfolds,
Of dreams that linger and whispers bold.

So close your eyes, drift away,
Let the spirits dance and sway.
In the arms of twilight's embrace,
Find solace in the endless space.

Secrets of the Eldertrees

Ancient boughs so wise and tall,
Guard the secrets shared by all.
Leaves rustle with tales of yore,
In their shade, the heart can soar.

Knotted roots in tangled earth,
Hold the whispers of each birth.
In the silence of the grove,
The tapestry of life is wove.

Sap that glimmers in the light,
Holds the stories of the night.
Branches sway with a gentle grace,
Caressing dreams in that sacred space.

Listen close, the wind will weave,
Tales of joy and tales that grieve.
Each secret held within the bark,
Guides the lost through the dark.

So wander near the Eldertrees,
Unlock their charm with gentle ease.
In every rustle, a promise blooms,
In every shadow, old magic looms.

Raindrops on Elder Leaves

Raindrops dance on emerald skin,
A gentle play where dreams begin.
Each bead a wish, a fleeting thought,
In nature's hands, the magic's caught.

Whispers drip from branches high,
Kissing petals as they sigh.
A symphony of soft refrains,
In droplets feeling no disdain.

Colors shimmer, shadows play,
Painting life in a dreamy array.
Elder leaves, like hands that cradle,
Nature's song sung without a ladle.

As puddles form on forest floors,
Mirrors reflecting ancient shores.
Each ripple tells a gentle tale,
Of winds that whisper, of storms that wail.

So let the rain bless all it meets,
In every drop, the heart repeats.
For within the pureness of the rain,
Lies the promise of joy after pain.

Shadows Dancing in the Twilight Glow

Beneath the dusk, shadows twine,
In a dance both fierce and fine.
Flickering lights in the charcoal skies,
Drawn by magic that never dies.

Whispers weave through branches bare,
Drawing dancers unaware.
Fleeting forms, they laugh and spin,
In the twilight where dreams begin.

As the sun sinks low and deep,
Night's embrace begins to creep.
In every shadow, stories loom,
Breathing life where shadows bloom.

Glimmers flicker, secrets sway,
Painting the world in shades of gray.
With every beat, hearts intertwine,
In the twilight's soft, warm shrine.

So linger long in night's embrace,
Find the magic in this space.
For shadows dancing softly show,
The beauty in the twilight glow.

Lore of the Ancient Canopy

In the shade of towering trees,
Secrets murmur with the breeze,
Whispers of the ages past,
Echoes in the shadows cast.

Leaves adorned with emerald hues,
Such tales in their silence bruise,
Of knights who roamed and fairies bright,
Guardians of the fading light.

Mossy carpets, soft as dreams,
Hold forgotten, timeless schemes,
While branches weave a quilt of lore,
That beckons souls to seek and soar.

Through dappled paths and breezy sighs,
Nature speaks while twilight lies,
With breaths of winds that twist and twine,
A symphony, both old and fine.

So linger here, where shadows play,
And let your heart begin to sway,
For in this ancient, vibrant sphere,
The magic waits, forever near.

Enchantments of the Whispering Glade

In the glade where whispers sigh,
Gentle breezes dance and fly,
Flowers bloom with vibrant grace,
Nature's heart in hidden place.

Moonlit paths where shadows hum,
Echoes of the night-time drum,
Stars adorn the velvet sky,
As secrets weave and softly fly.

A tapestry of dreams unfolds,
Of sylvan tales and treasures old,
Where magic wraps around the trees,
And time is lost upon the breeze.

Each creature pauses, holds its breath,
For life and dreams entwine in depth,
With every rustle, every glance,
The glade ignites a timeless dance.

So venture forth, let wonder guide,
Into the heart where dreams abide,
For in this glade, with whispers sweet,
The world of magic lies at your feet.

Tangles of Time in Nature's Embrace

In nature's hold, the moments blend,
With threads of time that twist and bend,
Each season's breath a silent song,
Where ages old, and new belong.

A blossom's bloom, a withered leaf,
In cycle vast, both joy and grief,
The sun and moon, they trace the years,
In laughter bright, and whispered tears.

The ancients speak in rustling grass,
In every storm, in every pass,
A tapestry of life unfolds,
In tangled roots and spirits bold.

As crickets chirp, and owls call,
The present weaves through past and all,
An endless dance, a magic thread,
Binding moments, alive and dead.

So walk the ways where shadows blend,
And take the path that seems to bend,
For in this realm, where time does soar,
You'll find the heart of evermore.

The Dance of Stars on Fallen Leaves

Upon the ground, a carpet spreads,
Beneath the trees where silence treads,
Fallen leaves, like jewels, shine,
A dance of stars, a tale divine.

Whispers rise with the evening mist,
In twilight's arms, the shadows twist,
Each leaf a story, softly spun,
Of days long past, of dreams begun.

With moonlight painting silver trails,
The nightingale sings, as magic sails,
Through rustling woods, the echoes chime,
In perfect rhythm, beyond time.

The stars above, a sparkling sea,
Reflect the whispers of what can be,
While fallen leaves, in colors bright,
Embrace the dreams that dance in flight.

So gather near, let wonder weave,
A tapestry for hearts that grieve,
For in the dance of leaves below,
A world of dreams begins to grow.

The Embrace of Shadows and Starlight

In the heart of the night, whispers weave,
A dance of the shadows that never leave.
Stars blink in mirth, their secrets unfold,
In the embrace of the dark, stories retold.

Moonlight bathes the earth in a silvery hue,
Where dreams intertwine and the old meets the new.
Stars serve as candles, guiding the lost,
In the realm of the night, no path is embossed.

Soft echoes of laughter, a soft rustling breeze,
A symphony played through the ancient trees.
Among the cool shadows, a flicker of light,
Signaling hope through the depths of the night.

Glimmers of magic where doubts fade away,
In the embrace of shadows, we find our way.
Each twinkle a promise, each sigh a prayer,
Under starlit dominion, there's beauty to share.

In this twilight realm, we learn to believe,
That even in darkness, the heart can achieve.
The shadows may whisper, but starlight is bold,
With secrets of night in their arms to behold.

Messages from the Woodland Spirits

Among the deep sighs of the ancient trees,
Whispers abound on the gentle breeze.
Woodland spirits dance in twilight's glow,
With secrets to tell, if only we'd know.

Elven laughter lingers in the air,
A melody woven with tender care.
They speak of the tales that the forests keep,
In hushed tones of magic, so wondrous and deep.

Mossy paths lead to their hidden glades,
Where sunlight dapples and shadows fade.
To hear their whispers, one must be still,
And open one's heart to the woodland's will.

Fingers of ivy entwine the old oak,
As spirit and nature join in the stroke.
Together they weave the fabric of day,
In messages carried by the woodland sway.

If you tread lightly, you may find a sign,
A glimmer of magic, the world so divine.
For the woodland spirits, both gentle and wise,
Look kindly upon those who open their eyes.

The Palette of the Twilight Realm

Brush strokes of twilight paint skies anew,
With colors of dreams, in the soft morning dew.
A canvas of whispers, where wishes take flight,
In the palette of dusk, hearts bloom in the light.

Hues of the night, a gentle embrace,
Where the stars lend their glow to this mystical space.
Each color a memory, each shade a song,
In the twilight realm, we all belong.

The horizon blurs where the day kisses night,
In the heart of the moment, the world feels just right.
Crimson and cobalt, a splash of the divine,
In every brushstroke, a secret, a sign.

As darkness unfurls like a silken spread,
The creatures of dreamland awaken, widespread.
In twilight's soft hues, we find solace known,
In colors of magic, we are never alone.

Tears of laughter blend with sighs of the past,
A tapestry woven where shadows are cast.
In the twilight realm, the heart spans the skies,
With the palette of dreams, the spirit shall rise.

Timeless Tales of Faery's Lullaby

In the hush of the night, soft lullabies sing,
From realms where the faeryfolk dance and take wing.
Whispers of wonders, tales filled with light,
Timeless and tender, they beckon the night.

Moonbeams like ribbons weave through the air,
While dreams fill the spaces, delicate and rare.
Each note of their song, a flicker of grace,
In the heart of the slumber, a warm, safe place.

As shadows surrender to dawn's gentle kiss,
The faery tales linger, a magical bliss.
Through fields lit by stars, where the wild roses grow,
They whisper enchantments in a lyrical flow.

Hold close these sweet stories, let your heart soar,
For faery's lullaby opens the door.
To realms of adventure, where wishes come true,
In tales of the timeless, a bond formed anew.

So close your eyes softly, let dreams weave tonight,
With faery's lullaby, your spirit takes flight.
In the world of enchantment, your heart shall abide,
Forever in wonder, with magic as guide.

Whispers in the Starlit Thicket

Beneath the veil of silver light,
Shadows dance, a ghostly sight.
Stars, they shimmer, soft and bright,
Whispers float through the cool night.

Branches sway with secrets old,
Stories of magic, softly told.
In the thicket, brave and bold,
Hearts of children, dreams unfold.

Moonbeams weave a gentle thread,
Guiding those who fear the dread.
In the dark, where few have tread,
Hope ignites, and courage fed.

Rustling leaves sing of the past,
Echoes linger, shadows cast.
In the magic, spells are cast,
To chase the fears that hold us fast.

Each step taken leads us near,
A world of wonder, wild and clear.
In the thicket, let go of fear,
Find the enchantment, ever dear.

Threads of Twilight Beneath Gnarled Branches

Twilight wraps the world in gold,
Gnarled branches, secrets hold.
A tapestry of tales retold,
In the twilight, hearts unfold.

Each shadow carries whispers deep,
Stories buried not to keep.
In the dusk where dreams dare leap,
Magic stirs from silent sleep.

Beneath the boughs, a glow appears,
Chasing away the doubts and fears.
With every breath, the night endears,
Woven tightly throughout the years.

Listen close, let silence reign,
Every sound a sweet refrain.
In this world, you can't explain,
Life's a puzzle, joy, and pain.

Threads of twilight, soft and fine,
Shape the future, intertwine.
In the heart, the stars align,
Beneath gnarled branches, dreams divine.

Echoes of Myth in a Hidden Grove

In a grove where shadows play,
Echoes of myth find their way.
Nature whispers, night holds sway,
Guiding travelers who stray.

Ancient tales on the wind ride,
In the stillness, dreams confide.
Mysteries that we cannot hide,
In this grove, our fears subside.

Moonlit paths invite the brave,
Through the thickets, magic pave.
Every rustle, every wave,
Lures the hearts of those who crave.

Beneath the stars, enchantments sing,
Creating sparkles, joy they bring.
Within the forest, wonders cling,
Tales of old, like flowers spring.

Harness the echoes, let them flow,
In this hidden grove, we grow.
Step by step, let your heart know,
Myths and magic intertwine so.

Secrets Woven in Moonlit Mist

In the mist where secrets lie,
Moonlight dances, whispers sigh.
Underneath the vast night sky,
Magic's breath will never die.

Silvery threads, like lace, entwine,
Softly glimmering, oh so fine.
In the shadows, hopes align,
Finding peace in the divine.

Every flicker tells a tale,
Of lost dreams and ships that sail.
Through the mist, where spirits trail,
Listen close, for love won't fail.

Woven tightly, history holds,
In moonlit tapestries, it unfolds.
Across the land, a magic molds,
In every heart, a story retold.

Secrets linger, calling near,
In this moment, crystal clear.
With each breath, you'll feel the cheer,
Moonlit mist forever dear.

Melodies from the Grove of Ancients

In whispers soft, the branches hum,
Ancient tales where shadows come.
Each rustling leaf, a note of grace,
Time's embrace in this sacred space.

Beneath the boughs, the spirits twirl,
With every breeze, a magic swirl.
The moonlight dances on damp earth,
Celebrating nature's rebirth.

Where roots entwine, a secret thread,
Binding dreams of those long dead.
A symphony of hearts beats strong,
In the darkness, they belong.

As larks take flight at break of day,
The grove will teach what words can't say.
For in each trunk, a history lies,
With echoes faint of lullabies.

So pause awhile, and listen near,
To earthly songs that charm the ear.
In every branch, a heartbeat lies,
Where ancient wood and starlight ties.

Sagas Woven in Arboreal Silence

In stillness deep, the forest sighs,
Unfolding tales of time gone by.
The bark of trees, a storybook,
In every knot, a secret nook.

Beneath the canopy's gentle sway,
The midnight stars come out to play.
With every rustle, stories bloom,
Casting shadows in the gloom.

An owl's soft hoot, a whispered lore,
Of moonlit paths and legends sore.
Through tangled vines and thicket wide,
The echoes of the past abide.

Each creature's path, a plot unfurls,
The dance of life, a swirl of worlds.
In dew-kissed morn, the daylight breaks,
Awakening all the dreams it makes.

In this embrace of ancient trees,
The spirit stirs upon the breeze.
Through arboreal echoes, we roam,
Finding our place in the woods called home.

Stories from the Edge of the World

At twilight's edge, where land meets sea,
Whispers weave where none can see.
The horizon holds a tale untold,
Of brave hearts, both young and old.

With waves that crash and wind that wails,
Adventures drift on salty trails.
Each star that twinkles in the night,
Calls out to those who dare take flight.

Upon the cliffs, the legends rise,
Of treasure hunts and daring skies.
In every stone, a history lies,
Echoes of youth, where freedom flies.

To sail beyond the maps we know,
To chase that dream with fiery glow.
For in each heart, a compass spins,
Guiding us where the journey begins.

So gather round, beneath the moon,
And hear the lull of ocean's tune.
For every wave, a story calls,
From the edge of worlds, where magic sprawls.

The Glow of Legends in the Canopy

In twilight dreams, the branches glow,
With tales of old, that softly flow.
Through emerald leaves, the stories dance,
Whispering secrets of chance and romance.

A flicker here, a shimmer bright,
The glow of legends soft as night.
With every rustle, the past is near,
Drawing close, we hold dear.

In twilight's hush, the creatures pause,
Reflecting life with winking jaws.
For every shadow holds a spark,
Guiding lost souls through the dark.

The canopy hums of magic's past,
Of dreams and wishes, forever cast.
With every breath, legends ignite,
Turning the mundane into the light.

So let us dwell in this hallowed space,
Find the glow in nature's embrace.
For in the woods, where wild things roam,
Legends shine, and we find home.

Epistles from the Forest's Heart

In the cradle of leaves, stories weave,
Murmurs of magic that never leave.
The whispers of willows, secrets unfold,
Tales of enchantment, forever retold.

Moonlight dances on shadows of trees,
Carrying dreams upon gentle breeze.
Each rustling branch speaks of yore,
A symphony soft, of legends in lore.

With every step on the mossy bed,
Echoes of creatures long thought dead.
In the depths of the wild, spirits abide,
Guardians of paths that the wanderers stride.

Amidst the ferns and the whispering pines,
Nature's embrace softly intertwines.
Here in this realm, all hearts are free,
To dance with the shadows, to simply be.

So listen intently, as night takes its form,
In the forest's heart, a quiet storm.
For in every sound, a story's heart beats,
A testament sweet where magic repeats.

The Saga of the Hidden Realm

Beneath the surface, a world in disguise,
Where secrets are traded for knowing eyes.
In shadows they gather, with starlight aglow,
Forgotten tales of the hidden below.

The flicker of lanterns, a guide through the dark,
Paths woven tightly, where whispers remark.
Each corner conceals a truth untold,
In the heart of the hidden, brave souls are bold.

With courage ignited, they venture in deep,
Through ancient corridors where shadows creep.
A saga unfolds, of courage and fear,
As the pulse of the secret world draws near.

A portal of wonder behind every door,
Echoes of voices from times before.
In this realm of dreams, where wishes are fanned,
Adventure awaits those who will stand.

So heed the call of the mystic unknown,
In the saga of shadows, your truth will be shown.
With every heartbeat, a journey in flight,
In the hidden embrace of the warm, gentle night.

Fragile Threads of Memory in Dappled Light

In the glimmers of sunlight, soft and rare,
Dance fragments of life, with stories to share.
Each moment a thread, woven fine and bright,
In the tapestry spun, of dappled light.

Whispers of laughter, carried on air,
Echo of childhood, unburdened by care.
Through time's gentle fingers, those echoes entwine,
Making fragile memories eternally shine.

In the garden of yesterdays, softly they sway,
The blossoms of moments, like petals in play.
Beneath the old oaks, where shadows domain,
Existence is captured in joy and in pain.

Each fleeting encounter, a spark in the mind,
Like rays through the leaves, beautifully aligned.
With every soft rustle, a heartbeat, a sigh,
In the fragile threads, reflections comply.

So cherish the echoes, the luminous flight,
Of memories' weave in the dappled light.
For in every moment, a treasure we find,
In the tender embrace of the soul intertwined.

Visions in the Garden of Whispers

In the garden of whispers, where dreams intertwine,
Nature's soft secrets in petals align.
The rustling leaves tell of journeys anew,
While sunlight and shadow paint vistas askew.

With each turn of the path, a glimpse of the past,
Visions unfurling, both tender and vast.
Here time stands still, as the moments take flight,
In the vibrant embrace of the day merging night.

The air is adorned with the scent of the rare,
Fleeting thoughts wandering through fragrant affair.
In whispers of blooms, a melody sings,
Casting forth wonders on soft, gentle wings.

Through thickets of dreams, hearts flutter and sway,
In the garden's embrace, the lost find their way.
For visions are planted in each flowering face,
A symphony sweet in nature's warm grace.

So linger awhile where the shadows entwine,
In the garden of whispers, let souls brightly shine.
For every soft whisper is a tale yet untold,
In the embrace of the blooms, where love is retold.

Lament of the Enchanted Glade

In shadows deep where whispers sigh,
The ancient trees in silence cry.
A stream flows gently, secrets told,
Of dreams once bright, now faint and cold.

The moonlight dances on the leaves,
With every rustle, the heart grieves.
For memories linger, bittersweet,
In the glade where lost souls meet.

The flowers wilt in mournful hues,
Their petals brushed by timeless dews.
Each step echoes, a soft refrain,
In this realm where love meets pain.

But hope's a spark in twilight's hand,
In the forest thick and grand.
With every breath, the spirits call,
In the enchanted glade where magic falls.

So listen close, oh traveler dear,
For in this place, the past draws near.
Through foliage thick, the tales unfold,
Of a glade wrapped in stories old.

Dances in the Luminous Underbrush

Beneath the boughs where fairies play,
In flickering light, night meets the day.
The underbrush alive with glee,
Twinkling bright, a jubilee.

With every rustle, shadows leap,
In the forest's heart, secrets keep.
A symphony of vibrant sound,
In this sacred space, joy is found.

Glowing mushrooms light the way,
As ancient spirits twirl and sway.
With laughter soft, they spin and glide,
In the warmth of night, they confide.

Amidst the leaves, sweet scents arise,
An echo of enchantment lies.
With shimmering wings and brightened eyes,
They dance beneath the starlit skies.

So wander forth, embrace the night,
In luminous dance, take your flight.
Through the underbrush, hearts run free,
In the forest's pulse, feel jubilee.

Breaths of the Ancient Wyvern

In cliffs so high where shadows loom,
An ancient beast weaves tales of gloom.
With wings outstretched, the winds obey,
The wyvern soars, at break of day.

Its breath ignites the early dawn,
Awakening life on the mossy lawn.
With scales of green and eyes like fire,
It guards the dreams that never tire.

Through valleys deep and rivers wide,
In whispered winds, the legends hide.
Of battles fought and treasures lost,
In echoes soft, they count the cost.

Yet in its gaze, there's wisdom deep,
A promise held, a vow to keep.
For every storm that shakes the land,
The wyvern stands, fierce and grand.

So raise your eyes, let spirits soar,
In ancient tales, forevermore.
With every breath, the legends thrive,
Breaths of the wyvern keep dreams alive.

Chasing Flickers Through the Foliage

In twilight's glow, a dance begins,
As fireflies weave through leafy pins.
Their tiny lights a fleeting chase,
In nature's arms, we find our place.

Each flicker bright, a starlet's wink,
Guiding footsteps, urging to think.
In rustling leaves, their laughter sings,
Of mysteries found in simple things.

Through tangled vines and shadows tall,
We chase the light, we heed the call.
With wonder wide, our hearts take flight,
In the embrace of dusk's soft light.

So dance with joy, let spirits soar,
Through foliage thick, we'll seek for more.
With every glow, a journey starts,
In nature's weave, we'll find our hearts.

The night unfolds, adventures gleam,
In the forest's arms, we dare to dream.
Chasing flickers, hand in hand,
In this enchanted, timeless land.

Threads of Fate among the Briar Thorns

In tangled woods where shadows play,
A thread unwinds in gentle sway.
Among the thorns, it weaves and twines,
A story waits, where fate aligns.

Whispers stir the evening air,
A promise hidden, bold and rare.
The briars guard what's yet to come,
While echoes hum a haunting drum.

The stars above, with watchful eyes,
Mark paths where fortune softly lies.
And in each prick of thorny stem,
Lives hope to rise beyond the hem.

With every step, the heart can hear,
The tales whispered, drawing near.
In secret groves, old dreams ignite,
As fate entwines in silver light.

So tread with care, through thick and thin,
For in these woods, we all begin.
With every thread and every wish,
Life dances close, through bark and brash.

The Hidden Harmonies of Nature's Voice

In rustling leaves, a song is spun,
A symphony of earth and sun.
Soft murmurs rise from creeks so clear,
Nature sings for all who hear.

The breeze carries a gentle tune,
Underneath the watchful moon.
Each blossom's sway, each insect's flight,
Adds notes to day, and dreams by night.

A chorus formed from every sound,
In every blade of grass unbound.
With laughter ripe in whispered air,
Harmony blooms, both bright and rare.

From mountain high to valley low,
Nature's heart begins to glow.
As moments meld, and silence falls,
In hidden realms, the magic calls.

So close your eyes and breathe it in,
Let nature's voice awaken kin.
For in this world, the music flies,
Binding earth and soul, where beauty lies.

Tokens of Time in the Underbrush

Amidst the ferns, the stories lie,
Each fallen leaf a whispered sigh.
Time's embrace weaves through the green,
In every shadow, fate is seen.

The underbrush, a treasure trove,
Of memories where silence roves.
Each twig and knoll tells tales anew,
Of days gone by and skies of blue.

Among the thickets, secrets stir,
Each rustle echoes, memories blur.
In this haven where none intrude,
Time unfolds, both meek and rude.

With gentle grace, the seasons blend,
As whispers twist around each bend.
The past is written in roots and stones,
In every nook, the heart intones.

So wander forth, through wild and free,
For tokens of time await thee.
In every brush of hand and glance,
The underworld invites the dance.

Glimmers of Past in the Woodland Mist

In morning's veil, the mist drifts low,
A shroud where glimmers softly glow.
With every breath, the past entwines,
In whispers lost, where memory shines.

The woodland breathes a tale once told,
Of dreams and wishes, young and old.
Each step reveals a fleeting trace,
Of life that danced through time and space.

Beneath the boughs, beneath the skies,
The echoes linger, truth belies.
Within the dew, bright spirits mingle,
In every fold, a magic tingle.

The ancients speak through rustling leaves,
Of hopes that dwelt in tangled eaves.
And as the sun begins to rise,
The past unfolds before our eyes.

So let the mist embrace your heart,
With every breath, play your part.
For in this realm of dreams and time,
The woodland sings in ancient rhyme.

Journeys through the Magic Den

In shadows deep, where whispers dwell,
The magic thrum, a gentle bell.
With flickering lights and hidden doors,
Adventure waits on winding shores.

A wand in hand, I dare to dream,
Through twisting paths, a moonlit beam.
Each step unveils a secret true,
In the den of magic, all things new.

With creatures rare and laughter bright,
The air is thick with pure delight.
A puzzle here, a riddle there,
In every heart, a magic flare.

The trees, they hum a tune so old,
Of tales untold, of dreams bold.
In every glance, a spark ignites,
Through journeys vast, by starry nights.

So come, my friend, take heed and tread,
In the magic den, where spirits spread.
For every path that we embrace,
Unfolds the dreams of time and space.

Celestial Threads in the Twilight

When evening drapes the world in gold,
And stories of the stars unfold.
A tapestry of dark and light,
Whispers the moon to the night.

On silken dreams, the starlight weaves,
Each thread a tale, as twilight breathes.
In cosmic dance, horizons blend,
Infinite worlds around the bend.

The constellations sing their song,
Of ancient lore where we belong.
With every twinkle, secrets share,
In the vast expanse, we lose our care.

Through celestial paths, our spirits soar,
With whispered hopes on the cosmic floor.
In quiet awe, we find our place,
Amongst the stars, we trace our grace.

So linger now, in twilight's arm,
Where magic lingers, smooth and warm.
For in the heavens, we're never lost,
Just threads of starlight, gently tossed.

The Lore Keeper's Sanctuary

In a chamber filled with dusty tomes,
Where ancient whispers weave like homes,
The lore keeper waits with a knowing glance,
In every page, a fated chance.

With ink-stained hands and wisdom vast,
He guards the tales of the very past.
Each legend breathes, each saga sings,
In his sanctuary, magic clings.

Through fables rich and knowledge deep,
The stories of old, he vows to keep.
A tapestry spun with threads of fate,
In every word, a world to create.

The echoes of history dance and play,
As shadows flicker in bright array.
With every moment, a lesson learned,
In the heart of the keeper, passion burned.

So step inside, take heed and learn,
Of truths revealed and hearts that yearn.
For in this space, where stories dwell,
The lore keeper holds the magic well.

Fables Found in Forgotten Places

In corners deep, where silence clings,
Fables dwell with hidden wings.
In forgotten nooks, they softly sigh,
A treasure trove where dreams lie high.

The stories linger, waiting still,
In every whisper, a heart to thrill.
Through ruins old and paths concealed,
The magic of legends is revealed.

In shadows cast by ancient trees,
Echoes of laughter ride the breeze.
With every step, a tale unfolds,
In forgotten places, adventure molds.

Through winding roads and crumbled stone,
A truth emerges, woven and sown.
With every breath, the past entwines,
In fables found, where mystery shines.

So venture forth, embrace the night,
In forgotten realms, seek out the light.
For in those tales, both lost and found,
The heartbeat of magic will resound.

Enchantment in the Forgotten Ferns

In shadows deep where whispers dwell,
The ferns hold secrets, cast a spell.
With dew like tears on emerald fronds,
They dance to tunes of ancient bonds.

Beneath the boughs, the breeze does sigh,
And dreams take flight on wings that fly.
Each rustling leaf, a tale untold,
Of magic spun in hues of gold.

The forest breathes in sighs of bliss,
With every step, a fleeting kiss.
Through winding paths, we lose our way,
In ferns where night and dreamers play.

A final glow, the glimmers fade,
In twilight's clutch, the shadows wade.
But in our hearts, the echo rings,
Of ferny realms where enchantment sings.

The Riddles of Burning Petals

When petals fall like whispered lies,
They weave a tale beneath the skies.
In crimson hues, a secret glows,
Of fleeting love and long-lost woes.

With every breeze, a riddle spun,
A dance of fire beneath the sun.
The garden sighs, in fragrant heat,
As hearts entwine in secret meet.

The petals whisper in the night,
Of dreams that flicker, dim yet bright.
They beckon forth the willing soul,
To find the answers, to be whole.

But heed the truths in layered hues,
For every heart has fickle views.
A riddle here, a puzzle there,
In burning petals, nothing's fair.

Flickering Tales of the Eldritch

In moonlit realms where shadows creep,
The eldritch tales weave dreams in sleep.
With flickering lights that dance and weave,
They spin the yarns that few believe.

A hollow sound, a distant call,
Across the ages, echoes fall.
With whispered names that chill the spine,
The secrets of the void confine.

A riddle spun in cosmic dust,
In silence deep, we place our trust.
The stars above in courses traced,
In flickering tales, the shadows faced.

Yet in the dark, a glimmer glows,
Of specters past and endless woes.
For every tale, a lesson learned,
In eldritch whispers, worlds are turned.

Reverie Beneath the Starry Canopy

Beneath the stars, where dreams take flight,
We wander through the velvet night.
In silver beams, the worlds collide,
In dreams and wishes dimly tied.

The twilight hums a soothing song,
Each moment felt, where we belong.
In every gaze, the heavens sigh,
For galaxies in silence lie.

A canopy of twinkling light,
Where hearts entwine and futures bright.
In reverie, the souls unite,
In whispered hopes, we claim the night.

Yet dawn will come, as all must do,
To chase away the depths of blue.
But in our hearts, the starlit glow,
Will guide us back where dreams still flow.

Tides of Stardust Among the Fangs

In the whispering night, the shadows play,
With stardust glimmering in the moon's ray.
Fangs of creatures lie in silent wait,
As tides of fate sway with an ancient weight.

On rocky shores where secrets dwell,
Echoes of magic weave a spell.
The dance of the waves, a haunting tune,
Guides the lost souls beneath the moon.

Beneath the sky, where constellations align,
The fangs of the night beckon divine.
With every tide, a promise is spun,
In the starlit embrace, we are all one.

Whispers of winds carry tales untold,
In the depths of darkness, the brave grow bold.
With hearts ablaze, we heed the call,
In the fangs of fate, we rise or fall.

With stardust dreams and a longing gaze,
We wander through this enchanted maze.
As tides shift and shadows wane,
Among the fangs, we seek the gain.

The Lure of Gossamer Dreams

In twilight's grasp, where dreams entwine,
Gossamer threads, so soft, divine.
They flutter like whispers on the breeze,
Enticing hearts with tender ease.

Underneath the veil of shimmering night,
The allure of dreams offers pure delight.
Floating like hopes, so fragile and bright,
In the embrace of soft, celestial light.

As stars flicker, beckoning near,
We dance in shadows, casting away fear.
With every sigh, a wish takes flight,
In gossamer realms of purest light.

Awake or asleep, the line is blurred,
In the gentle hush, our spirits stirred.
Where dreams drift softly, our hearts will roam,
In the weave of night, we find our home.

Let not the dawn break the spell we weave,
For in this world, it's hard to believe.
With gossamer dreams, our hearts conjoin,
In whispers of night, love finds its coin.

Souls Entwined in the Dragon's Nest

Amidst the mountains where shadows crawl,
In hidden caves, we hearken the call.
Souls entwined in a dance so bold,
Guarded by dragons, a legend unfolds.

Their fiery eyes, like embers aglow,
Watch over secrets that time shall bestow.
With wings unfurled, they soar through the night,
Guardians of dreams, fierce and light.

In the heart of the nest, where magic aligns,
Our spirits entwined like ancient twines.
With every heartbeat, the dragons roar,
Binding our souls to the tales of yore.

Whispers of courage in every flight,
Guide us through shadows and into the light.
In realms of wonder, we find our way,
In the dragon's embrace, forever we stay.

In the echoes of legends, our names shall be heard,
As we dance with the flames, unafraid, undeterred.
Within the dragon's nest, we dare to dream,
With souls entwined, forever we gleam.

Chronicles of the Elemental Thrum

In the heart of the earth, thrum songs arise,
Elemental whispers beneath boundless skies.
The dance of the waters, the fire's embrace,
Weaving the threads of time and space.

The air is alive with stories untold,
Of storms and calm, of the brave and bold.
Each breath we take, a note in the song,
In the chronicle's weave, we all belong.

With every heartbeat, the earth ignites,
Flames of passion, in our sights.
The thrum of life pulses, wild and free,
In elemental realms, we learn to be.

Rivers of silver and mountains of gold,
The chronicles echo through ages old.
With spirits united, we rise and soar,
Through the thrum of existence, forevermore.

So gather your dreams, let your heart expand,
In the elemental dance, take my hand.
We'll write our tales in the stars above,
In the chronicles of life, let's dance and love.

Moonlit Chronicles of the Lost

In shadows deep where secrets hide,
The moonlight casts its silver guide.
With every step on winding stones,
The tale of past in whispers tones.

A flicker here, a rustle there,
Soft echoes dance upon the air.
The forest breathes a mystic song,
Of wanderers who've roamed too long.

Their laughter lingers, soft and low,
In every glade where wild winds blow.
A tapestry of dreams unfurl,
In twilight's embrace, our hearts will twirl.

Through silvered woods with spirits weave,
The night conceals, yet dares us believe.
For in the dark, our hopes take flight,
In moonlit realms, we find our light.

The chronicles of tales untold,
In whispered winds, a courage bold.
So grasp the night, dear traveler lost,
For every dream, we pay the cost.

Reflections of a Whispering Dreamscape

In quiet corners of the mind,
Where visions bloom, we seek to find.
A tapestry of dreams unfurled,
In shimmering shades, a secret world.

With gentle brush, the stars align,
In reverie, the threads entwine.
The silent plea of hearts entreat,
In echoes soft, our dreams repeat.

Each whisper glows, a beacon bright,
Guiding us through the velvet night.
A dance of shadows, bright and brief,
In twilight's breath, we find relief.

The realms we wander, the paths we chase,
In whispered streams, we find our place.
As dreams dissolve in dawn's embrace,
Our hearts will linger, a loving trace.

Reflections dance in the starlit sea,
Of secret hopes and what might be.
So chase the echoes, let them rise,
In dreaming's grip, we touch the skies.

Enigmas Beneath the Celestial Canopy

Beneath the stars, in shadows cast,
Where mysteries of ages past.
A quiet pull, a longing glance,
Into the void, we fill with chance.

Each glimmer holds a story wide,
In cosmic song, and dreams reside.
The moon observes with watchful gaze,
While worlds unfold in mystic haze.

In stillness, secrets softly hum,
As night enfolds, our spirits come.
A riddle waits in every sigh,
Beneath the heavens, time slips by.

We wander forth on starlit trails,
Through veils of night, where magic hails.
A dance of fate with every spark,
In endless skies, we blaze our mark.

Enigmas twirl like autumn leaves,
In quiet moments, our heart believes.
So look above, let wonder reign,
In celestial dreams, we break the chain.

Mirthful Echoes of Forgotten Whispers

In playful sounds of autumn breeze,
The laughter lingers through the trees.
Each leaf a story, brightly spun,
In joyful hues, our hearts have won.

The echoes dance from hill to hill,
In whimsy's touch, our spirits thrill.
With every step, we chase the light,
In mirthful swirls, the world's so bright.

Forgotten tunes, a sweet refrain,
That stirs the heart like soft champagne.
A tapestry of joyful days,
In cherished mirth, our souls ablaze.

Through skies of blue and fields of gold,
The laughter shared, a love untold.
In every moment, joy persists,
A harmony that cannot be missed.

So lift your voice in celebration,
Embrace the joy, it's our creation.
With echoes sweet, let memories flow,
In mirthful hearts, our spirits grow.